Words and Beyond

JAANVI IYER

Presentation by *BookLeaf Publishing*

Web: www.bookleafpub.com

E-mail: info@bookleafpub.com

ISBN: 9789363310087

First edition 2024

ACKNOWLEDGEMENT

I would like to express my heartfelt gratitude to all those who have contributed to the creation of this anthology.

First and foremost, I extend my deepest appreciation to all the renowned authors whose works have stirred emotions, provoked thought, and inspired me to delve into the depths of my consciousness and excavate the buried truths and untold stories that lie within.

I am also indebted to my friends and family for their unwavering support and encouragement throughout this journey. Your belief in me has been a source of strength and inspiration.

I am grateful to the editors, designers, and publishing team who have worked tirelessly to bring this project to fruition. Your dedication and expertise have transformed words into art, and I am truly thankful for your contributions.

Finally, I extend my heartfelt thanks to the readers who embark on this journey with me. It is your curiosity, your passion for literature, and your willingness to explore the depths of human experience that make this endeavor worthwhile.

To all those who have played a part, large or small, in the creation of this anthology, I offer my deepest appreciation. May these pages serve as a testament to the beauty of human connection, and the enduring legacy of literature.

PREFACE

In writing this anthology, I embarked on a journey through the labyrinth of human relationships. Each piece within these pages is a fragment of the diverse tapestry that binds us together exploring the myriad facets of connection, love, and understanding. As I delved into the depths of human connection, I encountered moments of joy and sorrow, laughter and tears. I witnessed the resilience of the human spirit, the power of empathy, and the transformative nature of love. Through the lens of literature, I sought to capture the essence of these relationships, to illuminate the beauty and complexity that lies within each one.

This anthology is a tribute to the bonds that bind us together across time and space. I hope that within these pages, readers will find echoes of their own experiences, moments of recognition and revelation, and perhaps, a deeper understanding of the intricate web of connections that define our lives.

The Pursuit of Happiness

I wonder where happiness is
In a world filled with sadness.

Is there contentment in this world,
Or is it hidden in our brain that's curled?

Do you find happiness when you see others
smile,
For which you willingly walked an extra mile?

Are you happy when you win a game tough,
Or when you see a ray of hope in times rough?

Is there happiness in the future or the past,
Or in expensive cars that move fast?

Do you get happiness when you get good marks,
Or when you see a flock of white larks?

Do you find happiness when you see your mom,
Or while getting ready for the annual prom?

Do you find happiness when you unexpectedly
succeed,
Or transform someone's life with a good deed?

Choosing personal happiness is an exercise
futile,
Only a life lived for others is a life worthwhile.

After all, happiness is a state of mind,
It's not a right or an entitlement, it's one of a
kind.

The key to happiness is in living every minute
with love,
Unfailingly expressing your gratitude to the
Lord with a bow.

In the pursuit of happiness, let's not invite
sorrow,
Real happiness is 'NOW', think not of tomorrow.

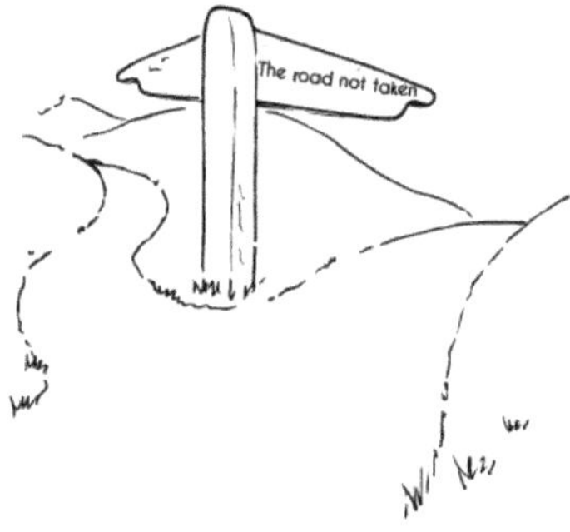

Dreams Unlimited

Dreams define your individuality,
Empowering you with wings to soar high.
Chasing aspirations brings you closer to reality,
Fulfilling ambitions makes it worth the try.

Dreams are not about building castles in the air.
But a deadly combination of courage and
perspiration.
Believe in your dreams and then seek to dare.
It won't be long before you reach your
destination.

I dream about being with my loved ones forever.
I dream about leading a life cool and calm.
I dream of spreading merriment, however,
I dream of making humanity a psalm.

Cease to dream and you cease to live.
As dreams propel you towards your vision,
Embrace your dream, make it your motive,
Not just a passing fancy but life's mission.

A heart without a dream is like a bird without
feathers.
Live your dream not that of others.
Succumb not to failures, don't quit.
Life's beauty is when dreams are knit.

A Man of Substance

A man who made a sea of difference in my life,
Who, without a grudge, bore all the strife.
Taught me to value everything I had,
Advised me to let go, and never to be sad.

'Mistakes are a part of growing up', he said,
'However, repeated irresponsibility will not be
tolerated.'
Leading by example was what he believed in.
Addiction to playing cards was considered a sin.

Always understood things from my perspective.
His coaching before exams was always
effective.
Though excited about his birthdays like a small
child,
He, never let his emotions, in our presence, run
wild.

He was my moral support, my pillar of strength.
As a fitness freak, he treasured his health.
Never was he desirous of accumulating wealth.
He always stood by me encouraging me to take
the big step without fear:
'Have no doubts, my child, as I am here'.

His early exit from that stage of life made me
wonder,
'Why did this man of substance, so easily
surrender?'
His absence has undoubtedly created a vacuum
in my heart.
Mere thoughts of this irreparable loss make my
eyes smart!

Emotional Turbulence

As the clouds came rolling dominating the
firmament,
A clap, a bolt tempered the celestial event.

Drops of heavenly water shook me out of my
reverie,
Flooding my heart with a painful memory.

As I sat beside the window on your rocking
chair,
Reliving the happy moments we used to share.

I saw your reading glasses by the bedside,
Questioning me why they were put aside.

Far away in the temple, I heard the bell clang
Reminiscing all the lullabies you sang.

A gentle breeze started blowing outside,
Tender trees dancing with pride.

A surge of emotions welled up in my heart,
Fate had undoubtedly played its part.

Everything was in place, but I found it in
disarray,
Silence is not golden as they say.

My eyes were looking for that special being,
Who could be addressed 'MOM' with feeling?

But life is all about moving on,
Experiencing the break of a new dawn.

The Bitter Truth

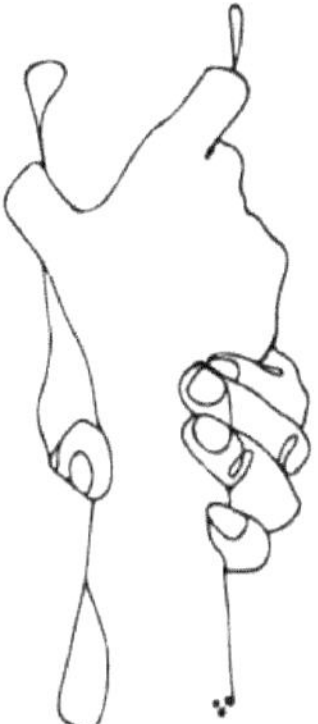

It has been a while since we have spoken,
It's weird but thinking of US makes me
heartbroken.

We have been apart for so long,
Making me wonder what exactly went wrong.

There hasn't been a word between us for days,
Is it because we chose to go separate ways?

The very mention of your name takes me down
the memory lane,
It refreshes my withered soul like a shower of
rain.

I miss your head on my shoulder, your hand in
mine,
Your enchanting smile made our togetherness
divine.

I fell in love with you the first time we met,
I thought it was instant chemistry, you bet.

The sound of your voice made my heart skip a
beat,
Every time I was with you, I felt so complete.

Within a short period, our proximity grew,
I was in a trance, my dream was about to come
true.

Was it just me who felt that way?
The consequences of which I had to pay.

As the distance between us started increasing,
The strong bond of our relationship started
weakening.

The passage of time made me realize,
Forcing you to hold on would be unwise.

After all, in your happiness lies mine,

God bless you, my dear, let your freedom be
thine.

I do not know if you feel the same as I do,
All I can say is 'I'll always be there for you'.

An Anchor in Disguise

A surreal feeling encompasses me,
An enigmatic ethereal vision I see.
A bright-eyed cherubin with her contagious
smile,
Cast a spell, hypnotizing me for a while.

A gurgling sound snapped me out of my trance,
With rhythmic moves, she began to prance.
Not containing myself I embraced innocence
personified,
With a shower of kisses my passion intensified.

Addressing me 'Mama' she dropped 'mana' on
the way,
In this state of Nirvana, I continued to stay.
Into a charming lass she grew,
The unique bond of love stronger as time flew.

Like a blooming bud her fragrance spread,
Transforming my life, she marched ahead.
When trials and tribulations bullied me to accept
defeat,
Her optimistic spirit made them bid a hasty
retreat.

Driving away all my melancholy with her presence,
She has taught me life's true essence.
With the sunshine of love she fills my dreary heart,
She is my Guardian Angel, My Counterpart.

Complex Transitions

It is a period of complex transitions, a period of
uncertainty,
Feelings so uncanny; with growth, comes
continuity.
It is mysterious why I am so bewildered,
With so many questions unanswered.

It is a divine feeling,
A merriment follows me,
But suddenly I break into a dilemma,
That corners me.

It is a giggle that escapes,
Transports me to seventh heaven.
But suddenly tears flow,
Into the melancholy that tears me apart.

It is a period of stress and storm,
A hesitant feeling that is the traditional norm.
But suddenly I desire to break the cordons,
That suffocate and strangle me.

A sudden urge to look within,
It continues to bog me down.
There is so much to endeavor,

The harsh realities of life are so profound.

It is a period of undue desires,
Pangs of muddled cravings follow me.
Suddenly I feel dragged into,
The arduous web that may never satiate me.

A sudden urge to love myself,
Create my own identity,
Strikes me and I know I thrive,
To make peace with ME.

A Change of Dynamics

In the dance of time, rhythm sways,
Dynamics shift in ever-changing ways.
Once firm ground now feels unsure.
As seasons shift, tides we endure,
Like whispering winds, emotions make us weak,
Transforming paths, we once did seek.

As I think of my guardian angel today,
The proximity we shared seems fading away.
Are we still on the same wavelength, I wonder;
Is my 'progressive parenting' a massive blunder?
Deep anguish has made its home in my heart
My forlorn soul has been ripped apart.

The fledgling I had nurtured is now scaling the
sky,
Exploring new avenues apparently gives her a
high.
Parading with the 'I, Me, Myself' placard,
Her confiding nature she chooses to discard.
Do we still share the same equation, the same
bond?
Declined calls, messages seen, but no inclination
to respond.

Long drawn silences have now become the
weekend highlight,
Jeopardizing our camaraderie that's nowhere in
sight,
Threatening to uproot the very foundation of our
attachment,
Trapping us in a whirlpool of baseless
disagreement.
The tenacious warrior in me cried out, 'Don't
wait',
Further added, 'Arise, Awake, before it's too
late.'

In-depth introspection blessed me with the
realization,
That relationships too have the maintenance
dimension.

Tempering them with the resilience to embrace adaptation,
Assists in an amicable millennial-gen alpha interaction.
For, as they say, in the flux lies beauty rare,
As old bonds break, new ones dare!

Reliving Childhood

As I sat by the windowsill after the chores were
all done,
Captivated by the enigma of the setting sun,
The sight of the echelons transported me back in
time,
Flashing cherished moments of life for no reason
or rhyme.

As the shroud of darkness cast its veil all
around,
My heart lit up with memories profound.
In the twinkling of an eye, blurred images
became clear,
Unforgettable moments spent with my near and
dear.

How can I ever disregard the incident when I
was kidnapped,
My presence of mind left my family members
zapped.
Being the talkative gregarious child with no
apprehension,
Be it any occasion, I was the center of attraction.

How can I ever forget my school which was my
sanctuary,
With sunlit classrooms that unraveled a new
mystery.
Casual acquaintances that transformed into
friendships strong,
Assisted me in exploring the path of knowledge
with the throng.
The enlightened faculty that empowered my
personality,
Deserve all the credit and appreciation with
utmost sincerity.

The annual summer break was a long-awaited
one.
Diurnal visits to the park were undoubtedly fun.
Pocket money saved for candies to be gorged on.
Small pleasures in life that kept the zeal on.

Mornings were spent on the terrace in the
sweltering heat,
Aiding my mother to make snacks was an
enjoyable retreat.
Binge-reading books of all genres post-lunch in
the noon,
Enhanced my vocabulary, I was, indeed, over the
moon.

Though years may pass, and pathways diverge,
In my heart, the childhood memories will surge.
Weaving recollections of that innocent phase
sublime.
Leaving indelible footprints in the sands of time.

An Ode to My Comrade

A bond so deep that it lights up my world,
Her contagious smile makes my joy two-fold.
With words like petals soft and kind,
She paints the canvas of my mind.
In her eyes, I see a reflection of our shared
history,
A bond unbroken, a timeless mystery.

Are you waiting impatiently for the name to be
unraveled
Of the person whose gracious nature is
unparalleled?
Well, she is my sister, my beacon bright.
Who stood by me through the darkest night.

In our late-night talks and hushed conversations,
We found solace in our shared confessions.
The secrets we shared, and the frivolous games
played,
Bound us together and a strong foundation was
laid.
In sunshine and storm, a confidant so true,
Her love and affection made me sail through.

With time, we may not meet as often as before,
But reminisce the remarkable days of the yore.
Even today, she has countless anecdotes to
share.
Her theatrical style of narration is indeed so rare.

So, here's to our eternal bond that's one of a
kind,
In every hue of life may our hearts always be
entwined.

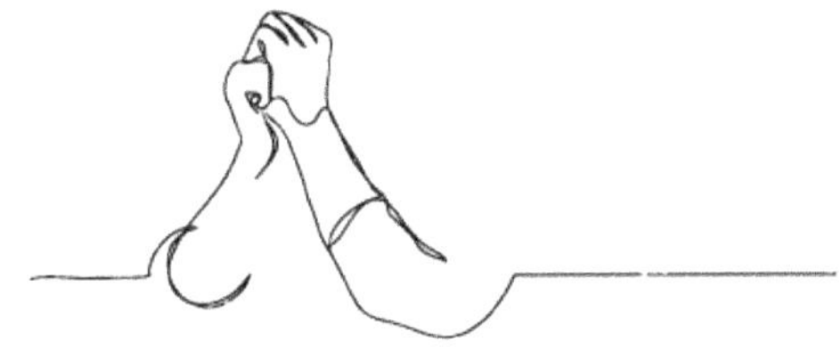

Bound by Blood

As I explore the intricacies of a unique bond,
That transcends beyond mere consanguinity,
I weave a tapestry of memories fond,
Characterized by a queer blend of love and
animosity.

Right from his birth, he was the cynosure of all
eyes.
The rebel in me wanted to break all the familial
ties.
But the mischievous gleam in his eyes melted
my core,
Brought out the hidden sisterly affection galore.

Pangs of jealousy soon took a backseat,
As I took on my quasi-parental role,
Nurturing him, I considered my feat.
Becoming his mentor nourished my soul.

Soon, a lifelong connection was built on mutual
understanding.
He helped me navigate through life's journey in
times challenging.
Through thick and thin, he was always by my
side.

His unwavering support helped me pass the tide.

In the ebb and flow of life's diverse range,
We find new purposes, priorities change.
However, time and space can't tear apart,
The threads of love that bind our heart.

My Ikigai

A pearly glow in the sky,
A graceful bow from darkness,
A standing ovation from light.

The rising sun cast a rosy hue,
The stirring of leaves, the chirping of birds,
Radiating vibrancy, refreshing hopes.

A serene aura, a celestial atmosphere,
For igniting young minds that have no fear.
Dark clouds of ignorance no longer appear.

Sharing my knowledge increased its value
manifold,
Thereby paving the path for hidden potentials to
unfold,

Empowering the future citizens with values to uphold.

My journey as a mentor has deeply enriched my life,
Interaction with my mentees, an antidote to my strife.
Teaching is, undoubtedly, my ikigai, my sacred art.
A legacy that is etched on my heart.

A Divine Mission

In the quiet, sometimes chaotic humdrum of the
classroom's embrace,
I have watched my tiny seedlings grow at their
pace.
Their angelic faces looking at me with awe,
Piqued with curiosity, concepts are still raw.

Their unconditional love is my greatest
achievement,
Propelling me to work harder for their
betterment.
From Shakespearean verses to modern prose,
From grammar rules and poetic rainbows,
We unraveled the intricacies of the language,
Appreciating its beauty in the course of the
voyage.

A mystic rapport was developed instantly,
A deep-rooted connection was brewing steadily.
Hand in hand, we traversed the path towards
enlightenment,
Exploring new avenues with unstoppable
excitement.

Handmade cards stirred the innermost feelings
in my heart.
Beautifully penned verses that made my eyes
smart.
The camaraderie we shared will always be
treasured,
As a memoir that will give us exultation
unmeasured.

As we bid adieu, let us not give room for fuss.
Let's look forward to the promising horizons that
await us.

Velocity- On the Move

A new start, a new beginning,
Life for me has changed in a twinkling.

An opportunity to explore,
Reinvent me to the core
Handle trepidations with ease
Sign up with confidence, for a long lease.

For years, I had caged my boundless ambitions,
Easily giving in to others' vile intentions.
Little did I realize what the consequences would
be,
Driving me to a state where I was not ME.

I began losing my control over my emotions,
Getting exhausted at the slightest exertions.
Words are more hurtful than wounds that bleed,
An understanding of my agony, my eyes did
plead.

My honor trampled in the sewers of crude
hearts,
My self-respect torn into innumerable parts.
I, suddenly, found the call of death appealing,
Such a disgusting journey was not worth living.

'Stop! Don't persecute yourself', said he.
'Such inclinations will never help thee.'
'You are too young to let such bruises bog you down.'
'Pick up the pieces of life, don't frown.'

Why not accept your worth in others' eyes?
Why should just being average suffice?
Why walk when you can leap?
Why not surpass your impediments steep?
Being slow and steady is an old version not updated,
Speed with direction is the new formula that's accepted.

Am I a Quitter?

I AM A QUITTER; I HAVE GIVEN UP
I don't think I can do it.
If you think I am a pessimist, I plead you to hear
me out.

I have quit talking.
Listening is a much sought-after art.
I have quit gossiping.
Ruining reputations breaks many a heart.

I have quit arguing.
My peace of mind is my priority.
I have quit judging.
I aim to spread positivity.

I have quit being bogged down by any
inhibition.
The more I struggle, the more I learn.
I have quit leading a life of self-deception.
Accepting reality is a welcome sojourn.

I have quit worrying about defeat.
After all, it is a stepping-stone to victory.
I have quit feeling lacking or incomplete.
My indomitable spirit will be MY STORY.

Love Unconditional

Unboxed, Unsaid, Untold,
Never did she let her emotions unfold

A mental turmoil ravaged her soul.
Her adorable persona it stole.

The bright smile that lit her face was just a
facade,
Concealing the scars that would never fade.
Putting on a happy mask that cloaked her
wounded heart,
Like a prima donna, she played her well-worn
part.

Myriad thoughts wanting to break free,
Waiting to go on an unveiling spree.
Suddenly a loud shrill cry broke the silence,
The time had come to go over the fence.
Unabashedly she made the complex decision to move on.
No longer would she endure the pain of being made a pawn.

As she began relishing her long-desired independence,
He walked into her life showering her with love immense.
His genuine care and affection made her alive.
The packaged pleasures in her began to thrive.
His courteous behavior swept her off her feet.
His presence, to her, was a soothing retreat.

In his arms, her soul was free to fly,
Savor and explore the limitless sky.
She had believed that 'Forever' was just an allegory.
But her PRINCE CHARMING had proved just the contrary.

Embrace ME

When asked to sum up myself in one word,
All I could think of was 'A Nerd'.
I wonder whether I know the real ME,
Or if I have molded myself into what the world
wants to see.

Many a time I have contemplated expressing my
viewpoint,
But refrained for the fear of being held at
gunpoint.

Throwing away my morals to be called 'Cool',
Is something that I loathe despite the ridicule.
Trying to please others has never been my forte.
Doing what is right is being 'Cool' in my way.

I am not afraid to go against the grain,
'Coz, I have embraced 'ME' to tackle the pain.

Behind Locked Doors

O.... innocent girl,
Keep your purity intact.
Don't darken your dazzling eyes,
For a world that's scarred and cracked.

O... sweet, adorable girl,
Keep your thoughts independent.
Don't let your thoughts be influenced,
By people in whom humanity is absent.

O... blithe, amiable girl,
Keep your infectious smile on your face.
Don't let them trample your happiness,
For it will hinder leading life at your pace.

O... flawless little girl,
Keep your soul immaculate.
Don't let them change who you are,
For being genuine today is a rare trait.

O... fragile little girl,
Keep your weaknesses veiled.
Don't show them your emotional side.
Always keep your demons jailed.

O... strong independent girl,
Take control of your life's symphony.
Don't let them write your destiny,
Interpret life as a CONUNDRUM OF
ESCORTICA.

The Assault

Darkness is like a horrifying curse,
Probably the worst topic to even pen a verse.
But there is a way to escape this complex net,
All you have to do is to understand your target.

Through darkness comes something bright,
The blessing that we call the miraculous ray of
light.
Where there is darkness, there is light,
Signifying that all is good and bright.

The creaky bones, the bad eyesight,
Yet the ability to turn wrong to right.
The world is pulling the weak in its might,

But to do good, we have to put up a fight.

Wars a-waging all around resides only pain,
Thoughtless vengeance for materialistic gain.
Innocent men, women, and children are slain,
Hope overcomes ill thoughts, peace will reign.

The Assault leaves its scars so profound,
Voices are stifled and dreams bound.
And then out of the blue, emerges a Saviour,
To save the globe from the Dark Side of Human
Behavior.

Blissful Bonds

In the trajectory of life, our associations play a
crucial role,
Giving meaning to our lives as a whole.

While the family forms the cornerstone of our
identity,
Our mentors play a pivotal role in shaping our
personality.

While some casual encounters do leave a
meaningful impact,
Deep and genuine friendships keep our sanity
intact.

Romantic connections are a concoction of
passion, fidelity and compliance,
Teaching us the intricacies of merging two lives
into a lifelong alliance.

Professional bonds foster a sense of purpose and
achievement,
Contributing to our overall sense of self-worth
and accomplishment.

The collective impact of all these associations
elevates human experience,
Instilling essential qualities of empathy,
compassion and resilience.

To keep the dynamics in relationships alive and
bright,
Nurture them with tenderness all day and night.

But as you keep the flame of love burning,
Don't get attached in the depths of longing,
For in the balance of give and take,
A possessive hold causes blissful bonds to
break.

Break the chains of close confinement, grant the
gift of space,
Let freedom find its place in love's gentle
embrace.

The Divine Connect

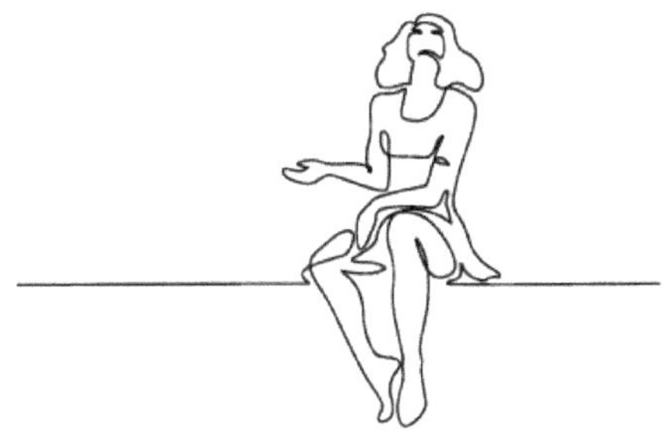

In the vast expanse of time and space,
Whenever I seek solace,
I sense a presence gentle and kind,
A love that's eternal, steadfast, and refined.

I believe there exists a benevolent force
watching over me,
Offering me comfort even in hours wee.
Alleviating my fears, soothing my anxieties,
Providing me hope when I grapple with
adversities.

Through fervent prayer and spiritual
contemplation,
I open myself to divine inspiration and
revelation,
Trusting I will receive guidance and clarity,
While navigating through life's nitty-gritty.

A heartfelt sense of surrender is fostered,
Control is relinquished, faith is empowered.

I recognize the divine spark within every
sentient being,
That serves as a catalyst for collective
well-being.

www.ingramcontent.com/pod-product-compliance
Lightning Source LLC
LaVergne TN
LVHW050940200726
843508LV00011B/2395